Let's Talk About
Early Language
Development

Let's Talk About Early Language Development

Ana Gamarra Hoover
Karen Griffin Roberts

Edited by M. Jean Buffardi

FOURTH LLOYD
PRODUCTIONS

Fourth Lloyd Productions, LLC
Burgess, VA

For permissions write to:
Fourth Lloyd Productions, LLC
512 Old Glebe Point Road
Burgess, VA 22432
email: stodart@kaballero.com
www.FourthLloydProductions.com

ISBN: 978-0-9889391-0-3
Library of Congress Control Number: 2013931796
Printed in the United States of America

TABLE OF CONTENTS

"Education commences at the mother's knee, and every word spoken within the hearing of little children tends towards the formation of character."

—Hosea Ballou

Acknowledgments

This book is written for and dedicated to the many families with whom each of us is privileged to work—side by side and heart-to-heart—during their children's early childhood language development. We thank you for your continued support as we strive to foster your children's first successful education experiences.

We are grateful to everyone who helped to advance this project. Our thanks to Mary Hanrahan, Jill Mcfarren Aviles, Stephanie Hanley, Karola Scarce and Margaret King-Sears for their reviews, advisements and encouragements. We especially thank Mary Fannin for finding and fixing grammar and typos after the three of us were convinced that the text was free of typographical errors. Ana and Karen are especially grateful to Jean for her patience, understanding and overview of speech and language matters to ensure technical correctness.

We would not have seen this book to fruition had it not been for the artwork, design and publishing advice received from Richard and Nancy Stodart of Fourth Lloyd Productions. Thanks also to our husbands, Rodger Hoover and David Roberts. Without their help we could not have met deadlines or answered countless e-mails while operating our busy households! Thank you.

Finally, we wish to acknowledge our "little ones" who inspire us every day. Each of you shares a special place in our hearts.

Foreword

As a new grandmother, I am remembering all the emotions of a first time parent: excitement, joy, and a bit of anxiety. As I did with my children, I want to see my granddaughter growing, developing, and reaching all the milestones of her physical, mental, emotional and social development.

Professionally, I am a college professor teaching the details of these early childhood development milestones to students earning degrees in early childhood development, to educators already working with young children, and, occasionally, to parents who enroll to learn more about their children. All of us work daily with this drive, this desire, to do the best for our young children.

We understand that communication is central to a child's social and emotional development. Yet, all parents and most teachers, if they admit it, have questions about what this development looks like, what the areas of concern are, and, most importantly, how to help all children develop good communication skills.

Let's Talk About Early Language Development is a gold mine of information about developing language and a great help for all parents and teachers of young children. In clear terms, the authors explain what the progression of language development is and how it relates to children's ages and stages of development.

We live in an increasingly diverse world, and parents of dual-language children may have concerns about how their children will progress in school. The authors use current research to reassure parents that preserving home language actually supports second language learning. Similarly, parents of children with delayed or absent language will be concerned about how to support their children's need to communicate. The authors provide clear information about possible reasons for these differences and practical suggestions for supporting each child's range of communication skills.

For teachers, this book is a wonderful overview of the context of children's language development. Children learn from their interactions with others—parents, teachers, other adults, and other children. Teachers need to be mindful of how language development progresses, and how to support the development of each individual child. Differences in the timetable and the ease of acquisition of language skills among children may provide challenges to teachers in meeting these needs. The suggestions of the authors for providing opportunities for children to practice skills in daily activities easily translate to classrooms as well as home. And when parents' and teachers' efforts complement each other, the child benefits that much more.

I really like the format of this book! Each chapter uses questions and answers to take seemingly complex aspects of language and explain them in ways that are both clear and practical. The authors' experience as teachers of young children means that they know, from their day-to-day contact with children and families, what questions and concerns parents and teachers have, and they know what strategies work best in helping children to progress in communication skills.

This is a book that I would not hesitate to recommend to any parent or teacher of young children. The information is up-to-date, accurate, and easily accessible to the reader. The resources and recommendations at the end are especially helpful to anyone wanting more information. *Let's Talk About Early Language Development* is a wonderful tool for supporting children's communication skills.

MARY D. HANRAHAN, M.ED.
Professor, Early Childhood Education
Northern Virginia Community College

Introduction

Let's Talk About Early Language Development is organized around real questions that we, as early childhood special education teachers, hear from our students' parents. We are intimately familiar with the concerns that arise when parents learn that their child's language is delayed.

Learning how to communicate is one of the most important achievements of early childhood development. Every parent eagerly waits for his child's first gesture, word, sentence, and writing achievement. When professionals discuss language, speech, and communication, they may seem to be grouping them as one-and-the-same. They are not the same, but they are so completely interconnected that they are learned together.

While the process appears common and ordinary, verbal speech is actually part of a complex communicative language process which is nurtured in a young child's environment by all of the people around him. Language is the basis for all communication, speech, and finally, literacy. A person can have language without speech and can have language and speech without functional communication. But, in all instances, language remains the source with which people send and receive information—the means by which we communicate with one another. Literacy is the final piece of the language continuum because it is fully dependent on a solid foundation of language and communication.

This book cannot possibly fully address all areas of language development, but we hope that as a brief introduction it will help families to better understand the many processes involved in developing early language for effective communication. We also hope that this book will encourage families to ask more questions and to understand the important role they also have in a child's development of language. Further, we hope this introduction leads to a desire to know more on this subject. We invite you then to review the recommended reading resources at the end of this book, which provide more detailed information on early childhood and language development.

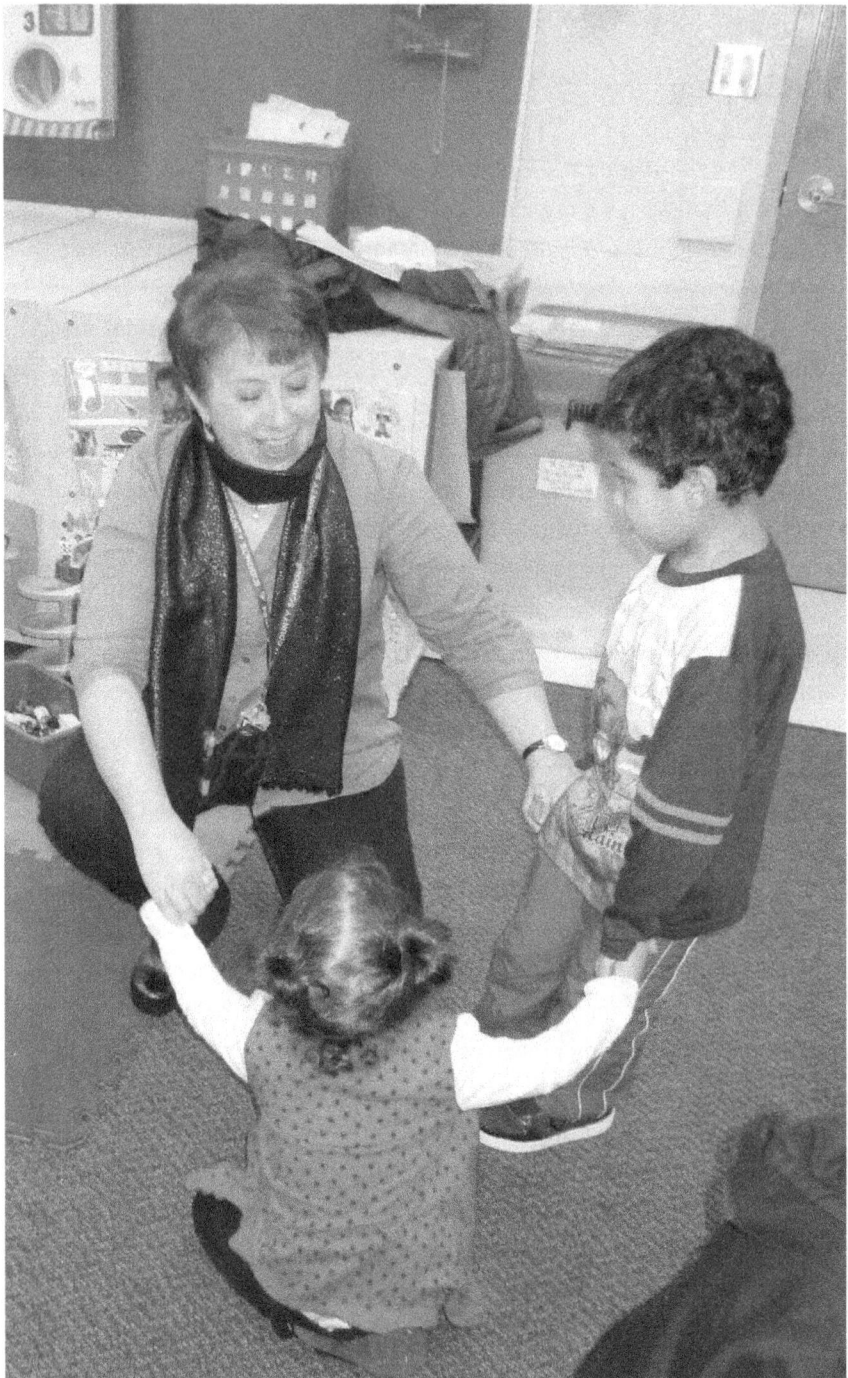

Chapter ONE

AGES AND STAGES OF
RECEPTIVE AND EXPRESSIVE LANGUAGE

How do I know if my child's language is or is not developing appropriately?

Language is indeed an area of development that may present itself at different times and in different ways with each individual child. Just as your child's pediatrician looks at his growth in height and weight and compares his size to an average of others his age, it is important that we track language development against an average of other children your child's age. Your child's first gesture, "Hi" or "Bye", your child's first attempt at speaking, or his first word, are important points of time in his language development. Specialists refer to these as "developmental milestones". Every child has his own pattern and pace for achieving these developmental milestones.

Let's begin answering your question by taking a quick look at what your child should understand (receptive language) and what your child should be able to gesture or verbalize (expressive language) for his age. A chart of developmental milestones based on these averages is shown on the following pages.

APPROXIMATE AGES AND STAGES OF EARLY RECEPTIVE AND EXPRESSIVE LANGUAGE
(Compiled from texts: Bee & Boyd, 2007; Shulman & Capone, 2010; Nekovel & Armis, 2006)

Age of the Child	Receptive Language — what is heard or understood	Expressive Language — what is gestured or spoken
Infant-3 Months	Attends to sounds, recognizes emotional tones, interprets speech signals, matches speech sounds to a speaker's mouth.	No verbal or purposeful gestures to communicate. Newborn's crying is his only means of communication. Fussing, gurgling, and satisfied sounds add to the crying and by one or two months the infant adds laughing and cooing sounds.
3-6 Months	Listens and continues to attend to sounds, recognizes emotional tones, interprets speech signals, matches speech sounds to a speaker's mouth.	"Coos" and may begin to "babble".
6-7 Months	May attend when hearing particular words combined with a visual preference, (i.e., "Mommy").	Adds more consonant (i.e. b,d,m) and vowel (a,e,i,o,u) sounds during vocal play, called babbling.
8-12 Months	Shows first signs that he understands the meaning of between 10 and 30 words spoken (or signed) to him.	Shows, gives, and points (with or without sounds) to call attention to something, to choose or request something, or to hear it named or see its use, such as a ball bouncing or a toy car moving. Babbling continues to about twelve months with strings of syllables such as yayayayaya-ya, dadadada.

APPROXIMATE AGES AND STAGES OF EARLY RECEPTIVE AND EXPRESSIVE LANGUAGE (CONT'D)

12-16 months	By thirteen months of age understands about 100 words. Points, looks, reaches for items or moves objects to show he understands what another person names. Gestures are often part of this early understanding, such as: "Wave bye-bye."	Jargons (combinations of sounds which may sound like words with intent to communicate to someone), gestures. First real "word". When prompted, waves bye-bye, hello, etc. Between 12-18 months of age begins to express about 30 words in his home language.
16-24 months	Continues to show understanding of new vocabulary weekly.	Rapid increase in verbal language! 16 months of age—average speaking vocabulary of around 50 words, and by 24 months an average of 320 words.
2-3 Years	Continues to understand new vocabulary and begins to refine the meanings.	Increases language to using an average of between 500 and 600 words by 2-1/2 years. After using 50 different single words, begins combining words on his own to communicate his own ideas or requests, such as "Momma sock" or "no cookie".
3-4 Years	Listens intently; begins to classify objects (types of food, toys, etc.) to link words to his real-world.	Generates beginning sentences and adds new vocabulary words to ask, answer and comment about experiences as they are happening.
5-6 Years	Can carry on a two-way conversation with peers and adults.	Uses a variety of sentences so he can easily communicate with peers and adults to make requests and comments, ask questions, and speak so he is understood. Says (+-)15,000 words.

Developmental milestone averages provide a way for us to track areas of significant delay. For example, if a child is three years old, says only fifty words and is just beginning to combine two words on his own, his language would be an area of concern, since this is language more typical of an 18-24 month old child.

As adults, we have been fully immersed in our language for so many years that we do not often reflect on the challenges young children may face during this important and complex stage of development. Young children are trying to learn the various aspects of language and communication just as they are learning other skills such as walking, eating, drawing, dressing, and playing in different situations. It is important to understand that many errors we hear in very young children's language are typical. In answer to your question, we look for errors that may not be typical.

What is meant by "typical" or "atypical" language?

Language development follows a certain progression beginning at birth. When a child's language develops according to an average level of other children his age—in the ways different aspects of language emerge—his language is considered "typical". However, if a child's language is NOT developing according to the expected progression, language would NOT be considered typical and would, therefore, be referred to as "atypical".

What should I do if I have concerns about my child's language development?

If you are concerned about your child's language development, the first thing to do is talk to your child's developmental physician. Ask to have both your child's hearing and sight checked. It is important for your child to be able to hear sounds and to see how communication looks among others.

If your physician shares your concern and there is no medical reason why your child's language is regressing or not progressing, you should contact your local government jurisdiction for family services. Every jurisdiction has a child services office. Some common names for the programs are: the Infant Toddler Connection (ITC), the Parent and Infant Education (PIE) program and/or preschool Child Find. Through these programs, your child can be evaluated for potential developmental delays. Once your child begins kindergarten, however, screening is done through your child's public school.

My child is already in preschool special education because he is using few words. Wouldn't he do better with speech classes to teach him how to talk?

If your child is enrolled, you are likely aware that preschool special education classrooms provide services to children with different levels of ability. However, to be eligible for special education services, there must be a documented delay in one or more areas of your child's development. Your child's teacher can help you better understand your child's specific developmental delays.

Your child's teacher may inform you that part of your child's developmental delay is in his language. Not meeting language milestones is complicated, because specialists categorize them specifically, as in: language delay, language disorder and/or speech disorder. A language delay indicates that a child is acquiring language in the typical progression but is acquiring his language at a much slower pace. A language disorder indicates that his language is progressing differently than is usual and is different than that of his peers. Speech disorder or delay often refers to a child who is difficult to understand because he is not able to "articulate" his words clearly, or he substitutes or omits speech sounds later than is usual for typical speech development.

Learning the cause of your child's communication challenges is a process in itself, because there are so many areas of language which should be investigated. While the underlying cause is not always identified, there are strategies which can help him develop his language. So that you might better understand the different aspects of language and communication, the following chapter outlines the five areas of language as they develop typically and atypically.

FIVE AREAS OF LANGUAGE

Pragmatics:
The social use of language

Semantics:
The learning of vocabulary
and the different meanings
of words

Syntax:
The sentence structure
of language

Morphology:
The smallest meaningful
units of language which
form words

Phonology:
The sound system
of language

Chapter TWO

Five Areas of Language

What are the different areas of language, and why is it important for me to look at these different areas?

There are five different areas of language, including: pragmatics, semantics, morphology, syntax, and phonology (Shulman & Capone, 2010). It is important to explore these areas because they help us to better understand typically developing aspects of speech and language compared to those areas which may not be typical. Special educators look at these different areas of language to determine where a child shows strength in language development and where a child may need support. Additionally, every language has a set of rules which determines what is expressed in socially appropriate ways and what is grammatically complete within a culture. People in each community have their own language rules in order to communicate successfully. Children acquire appropriate language when their communities and cultures guide them with their examples, interactions, and communicative responses. If a child is learning the language standards of his community, even if it is not typical of "mainstream" language, he is using language learning skills that show his capabilities to communicate in the same ways as those around him.

SOCIAL USE OF LANGUAGE (PRAGMATICS)

Pragmatic language is considered the "social use" of language. This includes the use of body language, gestures, appropriate social communication, the intent being communicated, and the amount of information given to a listener. Pragmatic language enables a child to convey a variety of intents, such as protests, requests, commands, questions, and comments about a topic. These are governed by rules that are learned through communication interactions in the child's family and community and may vary from family to family as well as from community to community.

Pragmatic behaviors also vary by situation and communication partner. For instance, I would speak to a child in a manner differently than I might address his parent. You would communicate with your friends much less formally at your home than you would communicate with less familiar coworkers at your workplace. To simplify this explanation somewhat, consider the different things one simple phrase can mean when social setting and body language are involved:

"Yes, I understand." (a child being disciplined)

"Yes, I understand." (a person learning what he needs to do next to collect his lottery winnings)

"Yes, I understand." (a teenager wearing headphones, listening to blaring music, and waving his parents on as he's getting instructions for what needs to be done while his parents are away)

"Yes, I understand." (a person called into the boss' office for his next assignment).

While the reply is the same, each one conveys a different social meaning within the context it is given.

Typical Development Of Pragmatics

Pragmatics begin long before a child is verbal (Greenspan & Wieder, 2006). Infants and toddlers use facial expressions such as smiles and frowns to express feelings and to react to those of others. They make eye contact and they make sounds in response to another person's sounds or speech. They use gestures such as nodding and pointing to help listeners understand their wants and needs. The ability to have ongoing back and forth communication, when two individuals are paying attention to the same thing, is called "joint attention". It is a critical part of language development. As adults interact with children, play, look at pictures, feed and bathe them, they are helping to establish joint attention as they talk about what is happening that both people are noticing.

An infant's communication is dependent on responses from the adults in his life (Shulman & Capone, 2010). When an infant cries, an adult comes to his aid. When a baby coos, the caretaker assumes the baby is content and might respond with a similar coo or a statement that describes how he thinks the baby feels. Around eight to twelve months of age, the infant begins to add gestures such as showing, giving, and pointing, with or without sounds, to call attention to something, to choose or request something, or to hear it named or see its use—such as a ball bouncing or a toy car moving.

As children become more verbal and reach preschool age, pragmatic language development continues as the child begins to use words and sentences to influence other people while he learns the social rules for language (Trawick-Smith, 2006). At this point, a child realizes his tone of voice and the way he phrases requests, protests, and comments are all as impor-tant as his choice of words. Children learn to initiate, maintain, and conclude conversations. They learn when to speak and when to be silent. They now have the ability to have ongoing, turn-taking communication about a topic in conversation with others.

Atypical Pragmatic Development

How can I know if my child is developing language atypically in the area of pragmatics?

At an early age, children with pragmatic delays may not use eye contact or gestures, such as pointing, to communicate. Young children with pragmatic deficits are not always able to understand body language or read social cues, so they may not know how to engage in social conversation. Because prag-matics involve the social side of language, children with some developmental delays, such as autism spectrum disorders, have different or specific difficulty with development in pragmatics. Children with pragmatic delays may be unaware whether another person is attending to the same thing they are in joint attention. They may have a difficult time initiating conversation, unless they need something or are otherwise highly motivated. Similarly, they often have difficulty adjusting their communication to different situations or to different listeners (Willis, 2006).

My son talks, so I know he has language and speech. However, his teacher says he has "non-functional communication". What does that mean?

Some children with pragmatic delays memorize particular phrases they've heard elsewhere and will continue to use those exact phrases in communication, although they may not seem relevant to the listener. Such phrases include partial scripts from movies, songs, or other communications.

Another area of delay in pragmatics occurs when a child is asked a question such as, "Where are you going?" and the child echoes the phrase in return, "Where are you going?", rather than directly answering the question. This is termed, "echolalia". While the child is taking a turn to talk in both of these examples, neither the echoed response nor the memorized response from a different situation is an effective communicative exchange.

As discussed earlier, a critical part of language development is joint attention—the ability to share with another person an interest about an object, event, or topic. Children who do not engage in joint attention have difficulty with the common uses of early language. They do not understand how others are attending to the same objects or information that they are. They might not understand how to direct another person's attention to something of interest. It is difficult for them to comment about an action or event and to know how to request information or clarification (Shulman and Capone, 2010).

If a child is not able to follow another person's eye gaze, point, or understand facial expressions and conversation about an object or event, he may not respond appropriately. Likewise, if he doesn't use eye contact, gestures or pointing, or comment about objects or activities with others, his communication with others is limited.

Without joint attention skills, children may talk about a favorite topic at every opportunity but resist exchanging ideas with others about their topics of interest. And, since they are not always able to understand how other people are feeling, children with inadequate pragmatic skills may not use words appropriately to protest.

Because these differences in responding interfere with the exchange of ideas and communication, you may hear special educators refer to repeated scripts, echolalia and the challenge of engaging in joint attention on a topic, as types of "non-functional communication".

What can I do if my child has difficulty using language to communicate with different people or in different situations?

Learning to read social cues

Social-emotional development is dependent upon positive inter-actions and communication with peers and adults. Since they often are unable to read social cues and understand others' feelings or intents, chil-dren with pragmatic delays are often excluded from interactions, and thus the opportunity to learn additional social skills through those interac-tions (Stanton-Chapman, Justice, Skibbe & Grant, 2007). Children who have difficulty with pragmatics need some assistance in interpreting social interactions.

You can facilitate social interaction by giving your child gestures or words to express his wants, needs, comments or feelings, and by teaching him the meaning of non-verbal conversation. For instance, when authentic emo-tions are happening, others can name the feeling and note the behavioral signs they use to identify the feeling. "I'm angry! or "_____ is angry! Look, his mouth is turned down. He's stomping his feet. He's yelling!" "_____ is happy! Look at his big smile! He is jumping up and down!" Family members are encouraged to share their expressions and feelings with each other so that your child gets to see representations of real expressions. Read stories on different emotions and point to the "happy child" in the book and ask your child to make a happy face along with other family members.

Playing with friends

Children with pragmatic language delays learn more through experiences driven by their interests and by problem solving (Greenspan & Weider, 2006). Peers are wonderful role models and can help involve children with pragmatic delays by playing games that require taking turns, such as rolling a ball back and forth, or taking turns stacking blocks. Role-playing about daily situations provides practice with the dialogue of different social situations, such as having family conversations, going to the store, or going to the doctor. This type of play gives children with pragmatic delays opportunities for both social interaction and communication.

Learning the give and take of communication

Reciprocal interactions can begin before your child says words. Rolling balls or cars back and forth, stirring something and then handing the spoon to your child to stir, or stacking blocks and handing a block to your child to add, gives him opportunities to experience the quick turns of interactions. Next, you can add words—make a one-word or short comment, and pause. The silence gives your child the message that it is his turn to say something—even if it is a sound rather than an identifiable word. Then, you can add another action and word that relates to your child. You can continue this learning process by modeling the different uses of language—to comment, to ask for information he wants, to request, to protest, or to greet. When these strategies are used throughout your child's day in ways he can understand and imitate, he begins to understand and develop the give and take of conversation.

It is important to interact with your child, to play, read, and look at pictures together. Take advantage of daily routines such as meal time and bath time to be sure your child is engaging in conversation and learning how to establish joint attention. Help draw your child's attention to things, to you and to other members of the family. Non-verbal gestures—such as pointing, reaching and nodding—should be used frequently to facilitate prompting of all children and to provide them opportunities to respond. Putting highly motivational items slightly out of reach of your child enables him to use his words or non-verbal communication to ask for the items, or comment on something two or more people are noticing (Koegel & Koegel, 2006).

Learning Words And Their Meaning (Semantics)

Typical Development Of Semantics

Semantics refers to learning vocabulary and the different meanings of words (Jennings, Caldwell & Lerner, 2006). Once children begin to talk, their vocabularies continue to expand as they learn about the world around them. Around his first birthday, a child begins to use his first words. Most of the words are nouns which he begins to categorize in some way (Goswami, 2004).

However, the child's understanding of a word's meaning may be too broad or too narrow. For example, a young child may call every animal with four legs a cat, because the first animal he ever saw with four legs was a cat. Later, he learns to distinguish specific characteristics about different animals to understand the differences. He might now understand that a cat says "Meow" and a dog says "Bow wow", but they both have four legs.

This type of learning involves all of a child's senses, including sight to see the physical differences between a cat and dog and sound to hear the differences in animal sounds. This is especially important because children must know both the spoken form of a word and the meaning of the word (Brackenbury & Pye, 2005). Experiences provided to children help them expand meanings so that the subtle distinctions in words are gradually understood.

Atypical Semantic Development

How can I know if my child is not developing vocabulary and different word meanings?

Children with atypical semantic development often take time to respond to or initiate verbal exchanges because they have difficulty retrieving information from their vocabularies (Shulman & Capone, 2010). While it is difficult to fully understand the reasons for these delays at a young age, they can possibly be due to slower general processing of information or limited organization of vocabulary. As a result, children may need more time to formulate words or may use very general words, such as "thing". Another explanation for a delay may be that a child has deficits in long or short term memory (Brackenbury & Pye, 2005).

Children with atypical or delayed semantic development often need

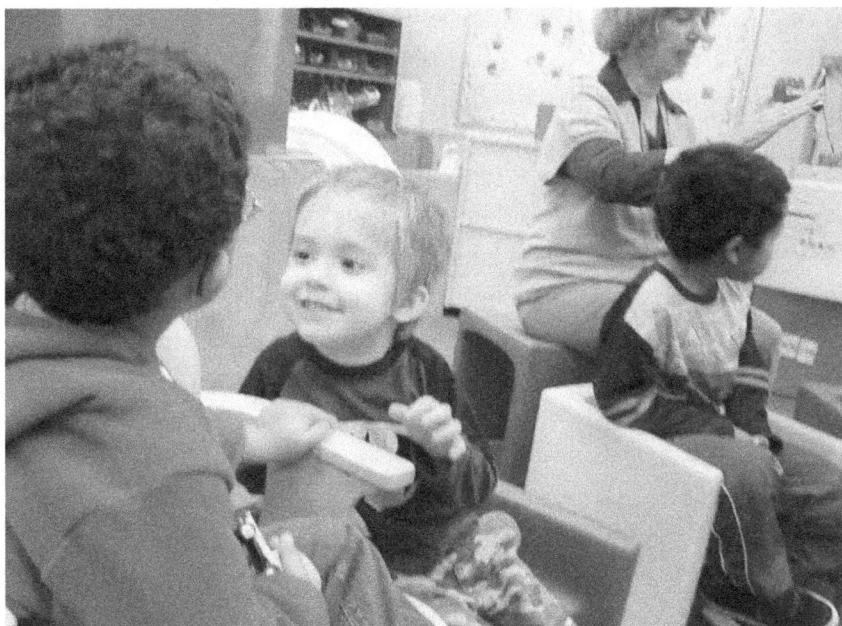

repeated exposure to a word, more chances to use the word, and more examples of the variations in the meaning of the word. Children with deficits in semantics may also begin to talk much later than their typically developing peers. They may acquire new vocabulary words more slowly and use words in more limited ways.

Some children with semantic deficits have vocabularies which are limited to facts that are well known and committed to memory. For instance, they may use the same word to describe more than its intent, which is typical for a much younger child (Shulman & Capone, 2010). They may use a word in circumstances where they first learned it, but then not generalize it to other situations or other meanings. In other instances, they may overgeneralize its meaning, such as calling an apple a "ball" because it is round and it rolls.

What can I do to meaningfully support my child's use of a variety of words?

Help increase vocabulary

Children with delays or atypical development of semantics need more examples of words and their meaning in different situations. Repeat words often during daily routines, play, and when reading books. Give many opportunities to hear and use words in different ways throughout the day.

When developing vocabulary, it is particularly important to your child that you include the sensory experiences (sound, sight, smell or feel) that are associated with a word. For example, an apple has a smell, shape, and taste. Using the same word(s) in different experiences adds to his practice and fine-tunes their meaning. Read books with your child. Name objects. Point out environmental print (road signs, restaurant signs, menus, etc.) and use words related to your child's activities to increase his understanding and use of vocabulary.

Engage your child in activities which help him have fun with words and assist in increasing his vocabulary (Bardige & Segal 2005). Some activities include: playing games with opposites, comparing objects, actions, textures, or people; finding things that are the same and different; and playing games with picture cards or objects of various categories that are natural to the situation.

Also, read books with the same word being used often in a variety of ways throughout the story so that your child can eventually fill it in. When a word might seem unfamiliar to your child, take the time to explain its meaning. Sing familiar songs, read poems, rhymes and change the words to focus on particular words. For example, a variation of "Wheels on the Bus" could include other vehicles with wheels. Singing "The wheels on the plane, train, truck or car" helps the child group these vehicles and practice using the specific name in a fun way. Using the same word and relating it to a real situation helps insure that it is indeed understood and that your child has the opportunity to use it many times.

Daily routines provide opportunities to categorize items. For example, laundry may be sorted into types of clothing, naming the item as you make stacks of shirts, socks, and pants with each addition. Continue this by adding other descriptors including sizes, the person whose clothing it is, colors, seasons (for warm weather, cold weather), or texture. Similarly, toys can be sorted into bins of vehicles, building toys, drawing tools, or toys for play food. Categorization of items physically may help your child group vocabulary words for later use.

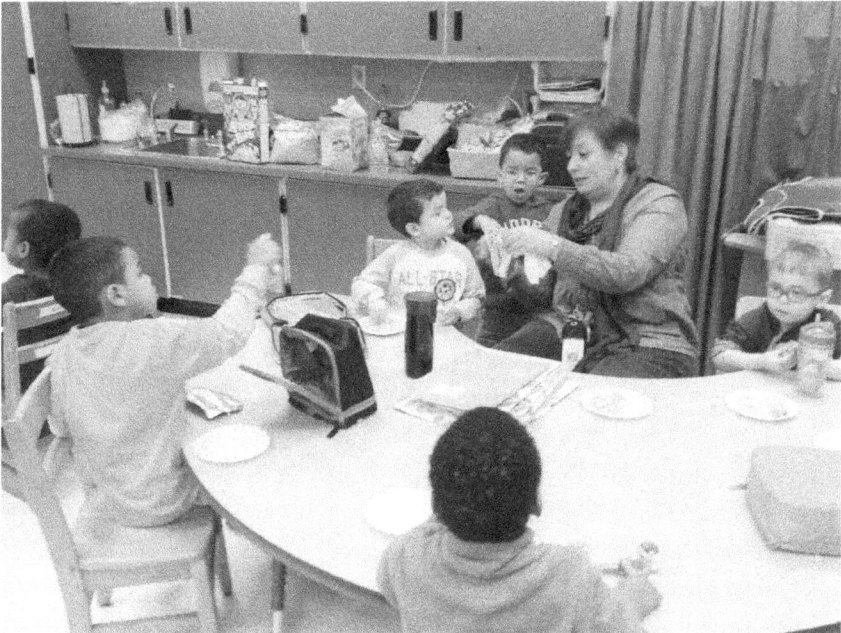

Meal times are rich in language opportunities. Foods may be named and described in a variety of ways, including who in the family prefers some foods. Your child could verbally ask other family members about choices for meals to provide opportunities to use the words. For example, your child could ask family members, "Do you want water or milk?", and then report back to you, "Johnny wants milk. I want water." Descriptions of temperature, texture, colors and tastes, such as salty or sweet, are salient while meals are being prepared and eaten.

Word Parts, Rules, And Sentence Structure (Morphology And Syntax)

Morphology is defined as the rule system of language for meaningful units, or morphemes, which form words or word parts (Jennings, Caldwell & Lerner, 2006). Morphology is the smallest meaningful unit of language. This includes root words (or "free morphemes") which stand on their own or "bound morphemes" which are sounds added to a word to change its meaning (Shulman & Capone, 2010). For example, begin with the root word "walk". When

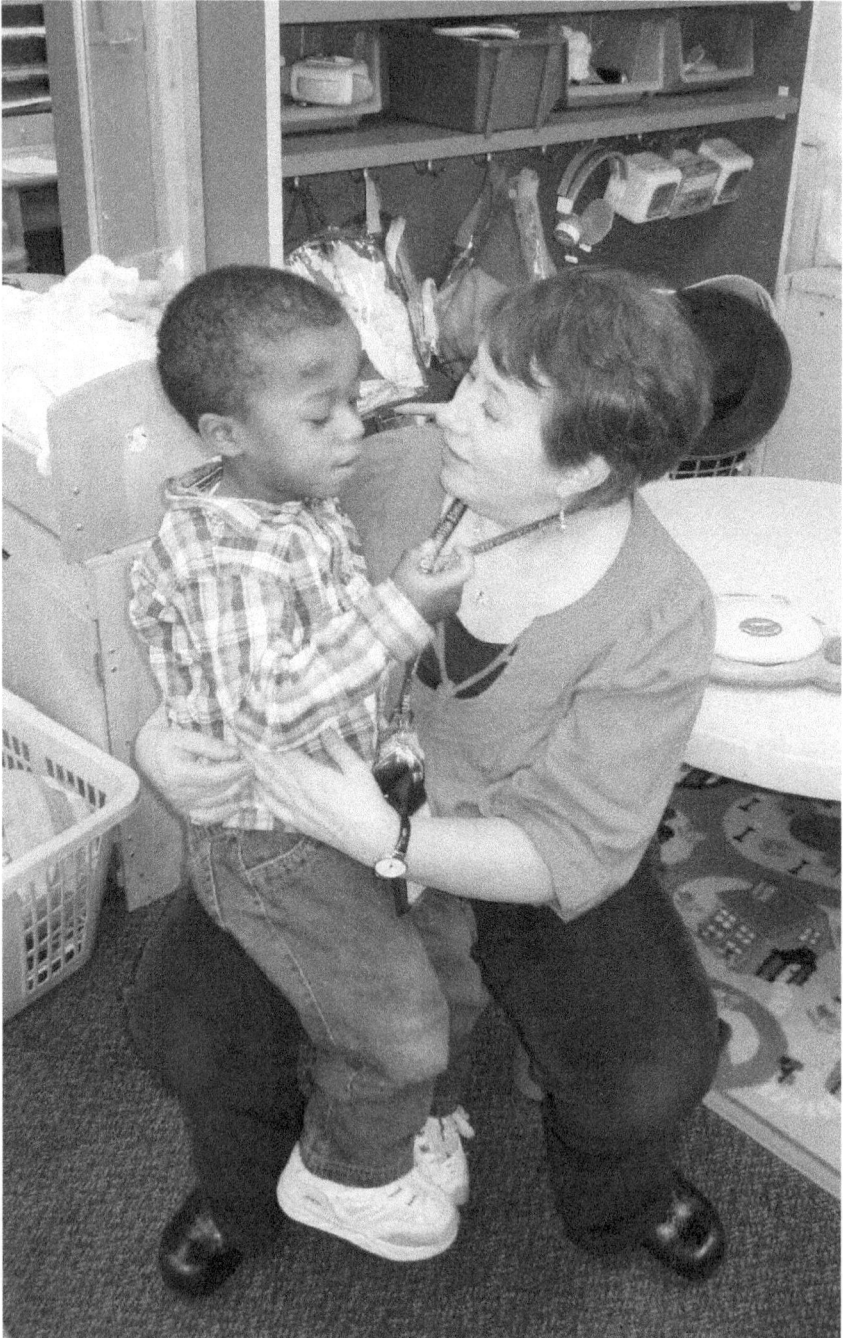

bound morphemes -ed or -ing are added—depending on the meaning the speaker wants to convey—walk then becomes walked or walking.

Syntax is the sentence structure of language (Shulman & Capone, 2010). This part of language determines the sequence of words so they have a specific meaning. For instance, in English "the cat chased the dog" means something very different than "the dog chased the cat." Different languages also order words differently. For example, while English puts the color word before the item (blue ball), other languages put the color word after the name of the item.

Typical Morphology/Syntax Development

Morphology and syntax begin when a child first starts to combine words (Shulman & Capone, 2010). However, what children learn about the rules depends on the specific rules of their language. Sometime during their second year, children who have at least fifty words will typically begin to put two words together. Combining two and three words to convey their own meaning is a critical stage of language development. The words they combine and use are usually those that are already in their single word vocabularies, and are then combined. Some word combinations may be learned as a whole, such as "thank you", but these are not indicative that the child is already generating his own two word combinations.

At this point in language development, context may be needed to understand the meaning. For example, if a toddler says, "Mommy sock", it might mean it is Mommy's sock. However, if he is getting dressed, he may want Mommy to help him put on his sock. "Sock off" might mean the sock is off or the child wants his sock taken off. The adult who responds to the child's intended meaning by adding a few words or word parts helps the child develop word order to clarify his communication.

Gradually, children use three-word combinations and then four-to-five words. These early word combinations or sentences begin with the words that carry the most meaning and are stressed, or emphasized, in the language. As adults respond with a few more words than the child says, the child gradually adds the unstressed words such as the English articles a, an, and the. While this process is happening, children are also adding word endings to convey plurals (dogs), possessives, ("Mommy's"), and tenses ("hopped, hopping") as they begin to develop skills in morphology.

During their preschool years, children are listening and learning the rules that adults or older children use in their home and community. First, when he is learning to talk about something that happened in the past, a child may learn the irregular form, such as "ran," because he hears it often. Then, he figures out that, in English, people around him usually add "-ed" to the end of actions that happened previously. Consequently, the child may say, "He runned after me." From others' responses to his sentence, the child finally sorts out when to use a word like "ran" or "ate" and when to use the -ed ending such as "jumped" and "picked" (Shulman & Capone, 2010).

Atypical Morphology/Syntax Development

How can I know if my child is not combining words or using grammatical parts of words as expected?

One of the most significant patterns which indicates a child is challenged using syntax or morphology (specific language impairment) is his difficulty using verb forms. In English, these might include is, are, am, do, can, and past tense -ed, and present third person singular s, as in "he talks" (National Research Council & Institute of Medicine, 2000). These patterns of impairment are identified despite having heard many examples of their use by other family members. Other features of syntax that may be delayed can include difficulty learning: articles (a, an, the); pronouns (I, me, you, your, him, his, he); plurals; but particularly, the use of verb forms (Leonard, 1998).

When there is difficulty acquiring syntax, instead of asking a question such as "Do you want to play?" a child might simplify to "You wanna play?" using the intonation to let the other person know he is asking a question. Similarly, a form that is typical of a younger child may persist, such as "Me not want milk" instead of "I don't want any milk." Instead of saying, "I am going" or "I'm going," the child might say, "I go." (National Research Council, 2000). If a child does indeed have a specific language impairment, this form of morphology may not be developed in his language even by the time he is school-aged.

What can I do if my child's language delays are found in the area of morphology/syntax?

There are a variety of strategies that can be used in daily conversations to provide opportunities for your child to increase his word combinations, to develop sentences, and to add word parts or grammar.

During daily activities or routines, include models of what your child might say in a particular situation. Then pause, while you wait for him to produce his own response. For example, if your child is pointing to a spill, you might say, "Uh oh, water".

It is important to provide a model without requiring your child to repeat it. The purpose is to clarify rather than "correct" his speech. For example, if your child comes up proudly to you and exclaims "I runned fast!" your response, "You ran really fast!" is affirming and clarifying about when to use "ran" and when to use the -ed ending.

Another strategy is expansion—when you add another word or two to what your child says. For example, when your child is rolling a ball and just says, "Ball," you might say "The ball rolls" or "Rolling the ball." If he adds, "Roll ball Daddy" as he rolls it to his father, his dad might reply as he returns it, "You rolled the ball to Daddy. I roll the ball to you (or child's name)" or "Daddy rolls the ball." These verbal expansions affirm your child's meaning and give him an example of the next step in development by providing a fuller sentence.

As indicated earlier, one of the most significant patterns for determining specific language impairment is a child's late or incomplete development of verb forms: particularly—is, are, am, do, can, the past tense (-ed) and the present third person singular (s), as in "he talks" (National Research Council & Institute of Medicine, 2000). You can assist your child with these verb forms by watching him in play and finding opportunities to help him develop vocabulary in all tenses. Commenting while your child is in play offers opportunities to engage in conversation with him and make him aware of words using action verbs, such as "You are building" (pause and wait for his comment). "You stacked blocks high!" (pause and wait for his comment). "I'm going to build, too" (pause for his comment). "I'm building a home. What are you building?"

Guessing games or questions and answers in daily situations also provide the extra examples your child may need. For example, after a shopping trip, you could put a treat in a bag and let your child guess. If your child asks,

"Gummies?" you can expand and model by saying, "You asked, 'Is it gummies?' No, it's not gummies." If he asks, "It candy?" you can respond, "Mmm (as if thinking) Is it candy? (looking in bag). No, it's not candy." If he asks, "Is it gum?" you can say, "Yes, it IS! It IS gum (pulling it out of the bag). It IS!" (giving it to the child). Then, your child can hide something so he can hear your questions in complete form in another fun exchange as you try to guess a treat he has hidden.

A similar scenario can be done when something your child wants is missing. During the search, you can model, "Is it under the chair? No, it isn't. It's not under the chair." If your child says, "bed," you can go to the bedroom and expand, "Is it under the bed? No, it's not there." When your child says, "In car" you can expand again with "Is it in the car? Let's go look. It IS! It IS in the car." The emphasis on words that don't carry as much meaning are appropriately emphasized in these circumstances.

Children's action and picture books also offer opportunities for focusing on the structure of sentences and verb tenses. Children's books with few words which repeat phrases also help children make sense of sentence structure. The pages might accompany descriptions of the picture, "He is playing... He is crying... He is building.... He is jumping." When you are reading the pages wait for your child to "fill in the blanks" and afterward model and exaggerate the appropriate verb tense.

The Sounds Of Language (Phonology)

Phonology is defined as the sound system of language (Jennings, Caldwell & Lerner, 2006). This part of language includes individual sounds and sound combinations which are heard in a particular language. Since phonology is based on a sound system, it is important that children can hear the distinctions in sounds, learn what differences among sounds are important to that language, and learn to produce the sounds to verbally communicate effectively.

Typical Phonological Development

Even before a child is able to speak his first true word, he has a strong perception of speech heard from others during daily conversations and care-taking (Shulman & Capone, 2010). From that period on, the infant begins to develop some speech and make the transition from babbling to speech. Speech perception is the foundation of phonology or the sounds which make up a language. Being able to understand the distinction of various sounds paves the way for effective communication.

Midway through their first year, infants begin to experiment with sounds as they begin to babble, playing with sounds. Later, at about the same age as they take their first steps, many will begin to say their first words. Just like first steps, first words are typical of children around the world and appear at about the age of twelve months. Early babbling is a first step toward the production of recognizable words.

A child's first attempted words are typically approximations of the true words. A child may produce simplified versions of words because he cannot yet use the refined movements to move tongue, jaw, and lips from one position to another to say all of the sounds in sequence. For example, bottle may become ba or baba (Shulman, & Capone, 2009). The child is also in the process of inducing the "rules" of the sounds system he hears around him. Families should understand that there are sound omissions, substitutions, and distortions which are typical for a preschool child who is just developing speech sounds in increasingly longer sequences. At first, children often pronounce just the first consonant sound and a vowel. Then, they might repeat that same sequence for a two syllable word, such as "Mama" for Mommy or "Buhbuh" for brother. Later, they begin to add an ending sound to short words, such as "hat" when they used to say just "ha", or "up" when they first just said "uh" to be picked up. Some typical speech sound substitutions include: the sound of a /w/ in place of an /l/ or an /r/ as in yewwo, for yellow, and haiwy for hairy or a /d/ instead of a /g/ as in "dum" for gum.

These speech sound substitutions are common and represent a problem only if they continue past the age when most children are using them regularly and/or they are heard in more words than would be expected, thus making the child's speech hard to understand. The average child should be understood fifty percent of the time by strangers by the time they are two years old, seventy-five percent of the time by three years of age and, typically, eighty to ninety percent of the time by age four.

Another step in development is called "jargon". A child strings together many sounds with intonation patterns that sound like a sentence. Sometimes they sound like a question, sometimes a comment, and sometimes a protest. The child is making eye contact with the intent to communicate. This stage is in contrast to when the child is playing with sounds in repetitive patterns during babbling for the joy of hearing and feeling the sounds. Sometimes when the children are using jargon, the listener can discern one or two words. Sometimes the whole meaning is unclear. This enables the child to "sound like" the others around him who speak primarily in longer and more complicated sentences and to take a turn in the conversation. If jargon is used longer than is usual or is used more often than is usual, it may be of concern.

Children typically develop different sounds at average developmental stages. Occasionally parents are concerned because their child is not producing certain sounds. Again, there are some average guidelines for speech sounds. These are given in the following chart, which outlines the appropriate ages when English speech sounds are produced in 90% of children (Virginia Department of Education, 2013).

Average Age	Female	Male
	APPROXIMATE AGES OF SPEECH SOUND PRODUCTION (90% OF CHILDREN)	
3 years	m, h-, w-, p, b, d,	m, n, h-, w-, p, b,
3.6 years	n, k, g, f-	t, d, k,f-
4 years	y-,(as in yes) t, tw, kw	g
4.6 years	th (as in that, feather)	
5 years	-f, v, l-, pl, bl, kl, gl, fl	y-, -f, v, tw, kw
6 years	th (as in thumb, with), sh, ch, j (as in job) -l	l-, pl, bl, kl, gl, fl
7 years	-ng, s, z, sp, st, sk, sm, sn, sw, sl, skw, spl	-ng, th (as in that, feather), s, z, sh, ch, j, -l, sp, st, sk, sm, sn, sw, sl, skw, spl
8 years	r-, -er, pr, br, tr, dr, kr, gr, fr	th (as in thumb, with), r-, -er, pr, br, tr, dr, kr, gr, fr
9 years	thr (as in three) spr, str, skr	thr (as in three), spr, str, skr

NOTE: letter with - indicates the sound is made either at the beginning or ending of a word. Examples: -ng would indicate at the end of the word, as in sang, and r- would be at the beginning of the word, as in rang.

Atypical Phonological Development

How do I know if my child's language is developing typically in the area of phonology?

For a child with phonological delay, development may progress in the usual order but slower than usual. His speech may be more difficult to

understand by those outside of his family than would be expected for his age. If the child uses patterns of speech sound changes that are not usual in the developmental sequence, it is described as atypical or disordered. For example, while it is usual for children to omit the last sound in words until about 2-½ years of age ("ha" for hat), it is not usual to leave off the beginning sound, such as "op" for "pop." In some cases, a child shows a strong sound preference and uses one or two sounds for many, such as /n/ for almost all consonant sounds while using the usual vowel sounds (a,e,i,o,u).

While it is typical to use sounds in the front of the mouth instead of those made in the back (such as "tup" for cup or "doe" for go), it is not usual to use sounds in the back of the mouth instead of those made in the front (such as "cub" for tub or "came" for same). Early in development, children may change one sound in the word to be more like another sound in the word, such as "pop" for "top" or "pot" or "momey" for monkey. However, these changes should be temporary. As the child is able to produce more fine movements with his lips, tongue, and jaw, and as the child becomes more familiar with the rule system for sounds of his home language, these sounds should be refined.

Finally, as indicated earlier, if jargon (stringing together many sounds with intonation patterns that sound like a sentence) is used longer than is usual or is used more often than is usual, it may be of concern. More in-depth observation may determine: if it's continued use is due to difficulty moving lips, tongue and jaw in refined ways; if a child has difficulty formulating the language; or if it is a normal stage and occurs only occasionally.

What can I do if my child's delays are found in the area of phonology?

To help children with phonological deficits such as when they are omitting or substituting sounds from spoken words, families can expose them to many opportunities to hear the sound modeled correctly and provide opportunities to repeat words with the age-appropriate sound. For instance, if your child has difficulty with the beginning sound /n/ as in "Ice kitty" you can restate what he said as a model such as, "Nice, kitty. He is a nice kitty" and by putting slight emphasis on the sound of /n/ (Shulman & Capone, 2010).

Choosing short words with sounds that are made in similar ways with age-appropriate sounds for emphasis is suggested to provide the best chance for success. Examples might be with the early emerging sounds such as /p,b,m/, that are all made with lips together. Early words might be Pooh (as in Winnie the Pooh), Pa, pea, bye, bow, bee, my, me, ma. Next, the same syllable is repeated such as: Papa, Mama, bye-bye. About the same time, a similar sound, such as pop, bop, boom, map, may be added at the end.

Next, the child is able to make a change in the vowels to say "Mommy" instead of "mama" or say "baby" clearly. Then, the child may be ready to change the ways different sounds are made within a word. For example, he can now produce a sound made with his lips at the beginning of the word and with his tongue at the end, such as in "pan" or "mat".

Choosing children's books which emphasize the missing sound provides you many opportunities to stress the sound your child may be ready to imitate. Read rhyming books, nursery rhymes, books to music or other children's books which focus on different sounds. As your child enjoys the rich sound-filled text, you are not only exposing him to hearing different sounds, but chances are, he may become so engaged that he'll make attempts at producing the sounds.

Chapter THREE

Dual-language Learners

Professionals often use the terms bilingual, dual-language, and English language learners (ELL) as if they were one and the same. However, there is quite a difference (Nemeth, 2012):

English Language Learners (ELL) are those who are learning to speak English, and little consideration is given to the cultural significance and importance of retaining their home language.

Bilingual people are fluent in both their home language and another language. This means that they are able to communicate, write and speak both languages fluently. Since very young children are all in the process of developing language, they are not considered bilingual. They have yet to master their home language, let alone a second language.

Dual-language Learners are in the developmental stages of learning two languages simultaneously (Nemeth, 2012). This book specifically addresses early language learners in the developmental stages of learning language. We consider each family's cultural influences on language. Thus, we agree that our young learners are "dual-language learners".

Our home language is not English. To help our child's language develop for school, should we speak to him only in English?

In the United States, dual-language children are most often learning a home language that is spoken by family members, while learning English in school and elsewhere outside of their home. We are often asked by families whose home language is other than English, "Should we speak only English to our child at home to ease his transition to school?" As special educators, our answer to this question is an emphatic **"NO!"** unless the family member teaching the child English is bilingual—able to communicate, write and speak both languages fluently.

Research suggests that children acquire a second language more efficiently if they have a firm grasp on their native language (Baca & Cervantes, 2004). It is so important for infants, toddlers, and preschool children to be exposed to language by family and community so that they are able to learn the processes necessary for communication. It is also important to understand that the rate of every child's language development differs with the amount of exposure he has to each language (Genesee, Paradis & Crago, 2004). While each individual has a unique timeline in the stages of second language acquisition, the developmental path is the same for ALL language learners (NCLR, 2005). Accordingly, we always advise families to continue speaking to their children in their home language. Children will learn English when they are immersed in the English-speaking community; they simply may need more time to hear and then practice using the English language.

By now you might be thinking how "daunting a task" learning two languages must be for young children! But remember, babies are born with a tremendous capacity for language. Infant studies indicate that they have the biological ability to acquire two languages as easily as learning one (Genesee, Paradis & Crago, 2004).

We now know that babies can distinguish different tones and stress patterns of speech in the earlier months of age. For instance, a baby can distinguish between a disapproving tone and a positive tone, no matter what language the person heard is speaking. As early as eight months of age, babies show a preference for language which is most often the language spoken by their mothers (Bee & Boyd, 2007).

While typically developing children acquire language in the first years of their lives and normally have basic language skills by the age of five, the process of language learning continues into adulthood. A second language can be learned at any age. Understanding a language depends on where the child is developmentally. Obviously, the older the child, the more intellectual capacity he will have to take on the challenge.

What if my child's English is not developing typically, simply because he is a dual-language learner?

It is NOT atypical to be a dual-language learner. Therefore, dual-language is not the cause of a language delay. Dual-language children with language delays will show the same patterns as children with delays who are learning one language (monolingual). Dual-language children with language delays will have *impairment in both languages.* Language delays and disorders are caused by biological or developmental factors which affect the entire language system (Nemeth, 2012).

Children with diagnosed disabilities are able to acquire two languages as well as monolingual children with similar abilities (Lowry, 2013). If children are exposed to a language-rich environment, dual-language children will reach developmental milestones at nearly the same rate as those of monolingual children. Because they are indeed learning two languages, there may be a slight delay in reaching those milestones, but often it is not cause for concern. Dual-language children may also have a slightly different pattern of development in certain areas, but only in the short term. For example, their vocabulary may seem more limited than that of monolingual children. However, by combining the number of words expressed in both languages, often the number of words a dual-language child knows in both languages averages the number of words known by a typical monolingual child.

Another common characteristic in dual-language speakers is mixing languages in order to communicate more effectively (Genesee, 1994). This is discussed further in the following area on semantics and dual-language learners.

How are dual-language learners affected by the different areas of language?

Pragmatics (the social use of language)

Each person is cultured by the many differences in communication in his social world, and each is, therefore, socialized into language (Genishi & Dyson, 2009). Differences in expression, body language and gestures in home cultures may not typically be seen in an English speaking culture. Children bring these first language experiences and cultures into the preschool classroom.

There are some cultures in which children are to be seen and not heard. They are not to speak unless they are first spoken to by an adult (Genesee, Paradis & Crago, 2004). In some cultures children are taught not to look directly at an adult during conversation. As indicated earlier, lack of eye gaze during communication is often considered an indication of a developmental delay. Cultural differences in families, in the mainstream community, or those used in the classroom, must therefore be taken into consideration for dual-language learners.

Semantics (words and their meaning)

Children who speak a language other than English at home are obviously developing vocabularies in their home language. As they are immersed in the English language, they build their vocabularies from words in English and their home language. As the child's vocabulary increases in each individual language, he learns to label concepts one-to-one and may avoid learning words in one language which have the same meaning in another language (Genesse, Paradis & Crago, 2009). And, since some languages have vocabulary words which are unique to their cultures or geographical areas— where they are most often spoken—there may not be a corresponding word in another language. As a result, the dual-language child might "mix" the languages by using certain words in his home language and other words in English. The dual-language learner may also learn the vocabulary of the home (family members, terms of endearment, furniture, foods, and clothing) in his home language and more academic vocabulary at school or in the community in English.

Phonology (the sounds of language)

Obviously, every language has unique differences in sound, but early development of phonology appears to be similar across languages (Genesee, Paradis & Crago, 2004). Atypical substitutions and distribution of various speech sounds appear to be similar in children whether English is their first or second language. The rules of the sound system of each language may affect one another. For example, if the home language does not typically use multi-syllable words, or does not add ending consonants, longer English words or the sounds on the end of English words may not develop as quickly with dual-language learners until both sound systems are acquired.

Morphology/Syntax (word parts, rules and sentence structure)

Limited uses of verb forms would not be typical for children whose home language is English after a certain age. However, it would be typical for dual-language learners to make grammatical errors when they are first learning to speak English. Dual-language learners acquire most of their English skills when they are socially immersed in the language. As they are exposed to different social situations, they begin to learn the skills for English sentence structure in their natural conversations (Genishi & Dyson, 2009).

The use of English sentence structure by dual-language learners may happen a bit later than that of their English speaking peers. However, if there is a specific language impairment, the child will have a difficult time with morphological or syntactic forms in both languages. He will need more examples and practice to acquire complete sentence structure in both languages.

What can I do if I feel strongly that my child is struggling with the English language because it is not our home language?

Maintaining home language is critical in preserving the family's cultural identity and supporting your child's self-confidence. Language is the most powerful tool we possess, and it plays a major role in supporting the process of forming your child's identity (Clark, 2009). Consider that your child's language

is as much a part of him as his name (Nemeth, 2012). Therefore, when a second language is introduced, a strong foundation in the home language enables the child to use what he knows about his language and to transfer skills from one language to another (Clark, 2009).

Parents will sometimes stop speaking with their child in their home language because they are concerned that their child will have problems speaking English in school. However, children are connected to all members of their family through their home language, and those special relationships can be compromised if you speak only your home language and your child speaks only English (Nemeth, 2012).

Ideally, all children should be in a classroom with home language support. Unfortunately, this is not always possible. As teachers, we encourage you to share information with your child's teachers about languages spoken at home, about traditions, celebrations, activities, music, games and food (Nemeth, 2012). You might also consider volunteering in the classroom and introducing teachers and children to your customs and traditions. Share recordings of music and songs in your language and culture.

You can also assist in your dual-language learner's development by reading to him. Reading in one's home language is important. Bilingual books can be obtained from teachers and local libraries, and you can request to have books translated into your home language. Talk about the pictures with your child in your home language, even if the text is written in English. Share storytelling with your child. Sing songs and play interactive games that encourage language. Use labels on objects around the house so that your child begins to recognize print and thus adds words to his vocabulary. Ask your child's teachers to help by providing the English word for those objects so that your child is exposed to meaningful print in both languages. Also, familiarize him with his spoken and written name in both languages. This preserves the home language and your child's identity, while exposing him to meaningful print.

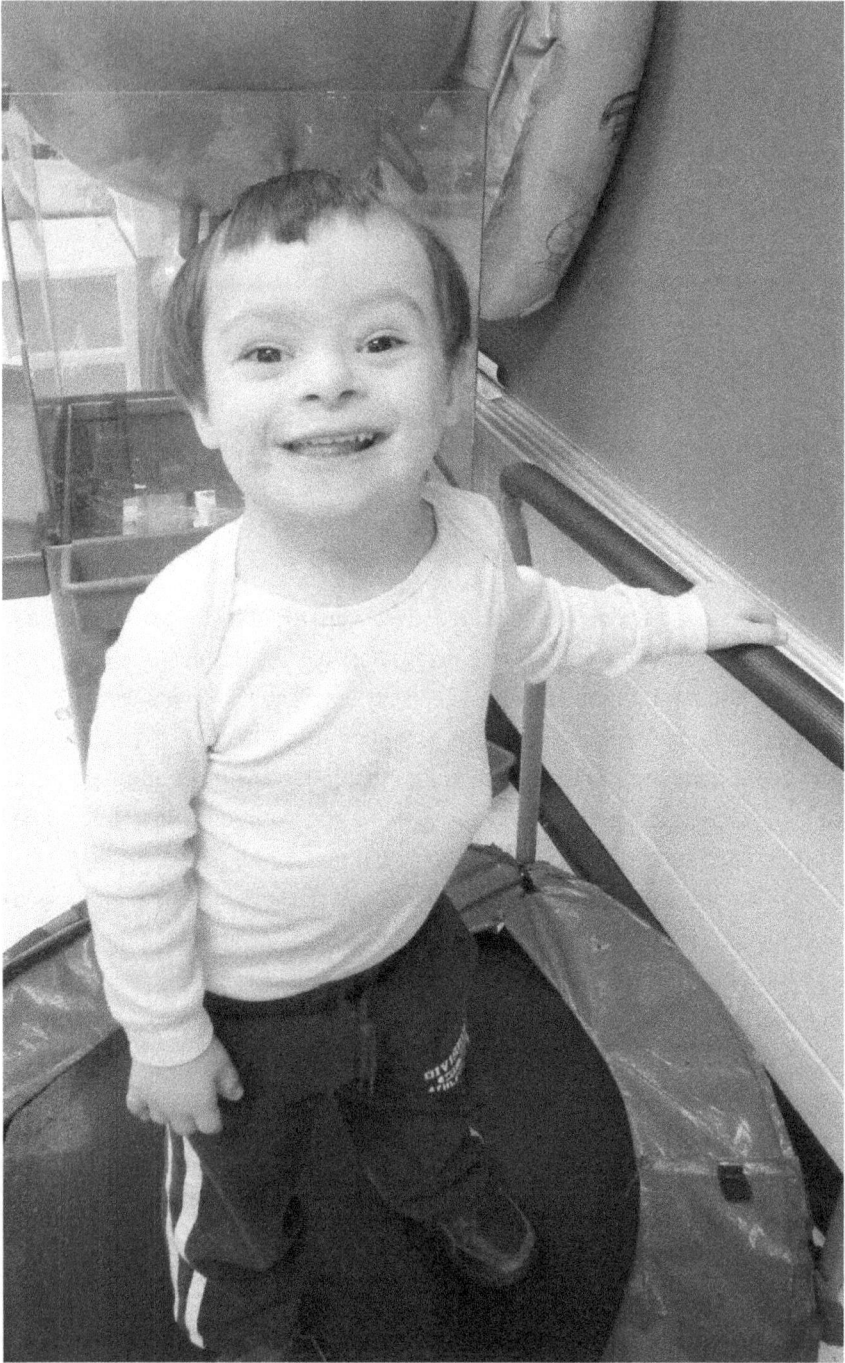

Chapter FOUR

Non-verbal Children

What can you tell me about children who do not talk at all?

We have many non-verbal children in our preschool special education classrooms. Some students enter our classrooms and their parents report that they spoke some words but stopped speaking altogether around their second birthday. This is a developmental trait that sometimes occurs in the history of children on the autism spectrum. Other parents report that their children have never spoken. We also see children who do speak, but, as outlined in the pragmatic language section, their speech is non-functional because they are repeating things that they have memorized, or they are echoing another person's question rather than answering the question.

First, it is important to remember that ALL social communication is not verbal. Recall the differences in meaning when body language and gestures were added to the example of "Yes, I understand" for pragmatic language in Chapter Two. Non-verbal children must depend on gestures and body language to get what they need, to ask a question, or to protest.

When a non-verbal child needs something, he often has to resort to tantrums or aggressive behavior to have his needs met. Unfortunately, we often first begin to understand what a non-verbal child wants *after* his behavior becomes sufficiently aberrant that we are considering behavior therapy. Once we've witnessed a child exhibit a 20 minute crying spree, and/or temper tantrum, or we've been bitten, kicked and hit a few times, we begin

to realize he is trying to tell us something! Can you blame him when he has exhausted all attempts at getting our attention to his needs that he uses what's worked before—quickly and efficiently—to communicate his needs? It is the responsibility of families, teachers and other professionals to help non-verbal children learn appropriate ways to communicate.

My child does not speak. Why? Will he learn to talk?

These are questions we are often asked by families. However, your child's medical team would be the best group of people to help you learn the answers to both of these questions. Every child's language development is unique, and there are many variables which affect if and when children speak.

Selective Mutism

I've heard the term, "selective mutism". Could that be the reason my child doesn't talk?

Selective mutism is a condition which is more common in children under five years old. A child with selective mutism is able to understand and can speak, but he does not speak in certain settings and environments. Again, the cause is unknown, but many children with selective mutism are thought to be over-anxious and/or may have some kind of phobia in various situations. Children with this condition are usually able to speak at home with family but exhibit fear or anxiety around people they do not know well. As the term implies, they are selective about the situations or about the people with whom they choose to speak (National Institutes of Health, 2013).

How can I help my non-verbal child communicate?

There are many ways to communicate without talking. In the classroom we try to use all means of communication with our children. We use very basic sign language, picture communication cards, prompts with simple gestures, repeated verbal and visual prompts and assistive technology. Teachers are always more than happy to share with you the strategies they are using in the classroom to help your child communicate, so please ask. In addition to the things we do in the classroom, here are some things you can do at home.

First, you must *always expect that your child will communicate.* Just as when you anticipated your child's first smile, roll over, crawl and walk, you should anticipate language and proceed with all of the strategies used for every child's successful language development. Give him words. Give pauses and time for him to respond in some way. Talk to him about what is happening during his day. If your child wants something, wait for him to request it by pointing or otherwise communicating to you what he wants. Too often when parents understand what their child wants, they will offer things to them rather than wait for a request. If your child never has to ask for help, he may not ask for assistance, and you will have missed many opportunities to help him develop some very basic communication skills.

Learn to recognize your child's non-verbal actions. For instance, when your child takes your hand and guides you to the kitchen, talk to him. Say, " You're taking me to the kitchen. Maybe you're hungry." After watching your child, perhaps offer him a choice. Ask, "Do you want crackers or pretzels?" while holding the two items of choice. Even if you know what he wants, wait for him to gesture, point, or otherwise communicate what he wants.

When your child is angry and is losing self-control because he cannot communicate, wait until he's calm and then give him words or choices about what you understand is his perception of what happened. Include context cues. Help him to recognize that you understand and acknowledge his feel-

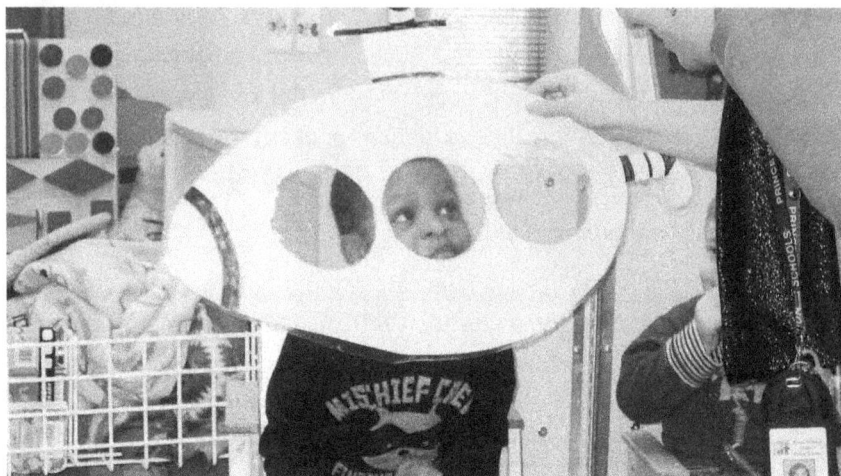

ings. "You were angry. You wanted to stay outside." "You are hungry! Do you want crackers or bread?" (showing both items).

Through body language and facial expressions, most children can interpret how another person is feeling. However, many children with developmental delays and who do not speak, also have deficits in social skills and do not understand social cues. They need specific and direct instruction on what they need to do to fit in their social environment (Howley & Arnold, 2006). When we discussed deficits in pragmatic language in Chapter Two, you may recall we outlined strategies to help your child learn about social cues. Take some time to review and practice some of those strategies to teach your child to better understand and develop some pragmatic language skills.

Finally, just because your child does not speak, this does not mean he does not hear you. In fact, he likely hears and understands more than you may realize. Your child has feelings, though he cannot always express them. He does hear you if you talk about his language challenges in front of him. When speaking about him with others use descriptions that encourage him, and save expressions of concern for when he is not within hearing range.

Chapter FIVE

Language, Early Literacy And Beyond

What about early literacy skills? Shouldn't my child know his alphabet before he starts kindergarten?

At this time, when elementary schools are driven by academic testing standards and scores, we are intimately aware of the anxiety felt by preschool parents. Questions abound: Does he know his alphabet? Does he read and write his own name? What can I do at home to help him learn to read before he starts kindergarten? He doesn't know his alphabet; should I retain him? Wouldn't he do better with another year of preschool?

Allow us to review an opening statement in our introduction: "Language is the basis for all communication, speech, and finally, literacy." A person can have language without speech and can have language and speech without functional communication. But, in all instances, language remains the source of the information from which people send and receive information to communicate with one another. Literacy is the final piece of the language continuum because it is fully dependent on a solid foundation of language and communication.

Before your child is able to make sense of the alphabet, the meaning of letters and their sounds, words, and sentences, he has to have a solid language base. For instance, most children can sing the alphabet in order by memory. But to the preschool child, "ABC's" is just another song they know and love

to sing. The letters are simply pictures to accompany the song, much like a star in the sky is the picture which accompanies "Twinkle, Twinkle, Little Star". *To them*, it makes perfect sense just as it is; they love to "read the pictures".

Once they begin to understand that letters connect to make sounds and sounds connect to make words and then words connect to make sentences, it is as if the proverbial "light goes on". They begin to read and write in a way that makes sense *to those of us* who have learned to depend on text. This is yet another magical moment in early childhood development.

Can I help my child develop early literacy skills?

Yes. Just as language begins at home, so does early literacy. There are many ways you can help your child develop literacy skills with the goal of him becoming a competent writer and reader. Here are some strategies that can be included as you play with your child:

> **Give your child opportunities to participate in the story telling** when you are reading stories. Talk about the book before, during and after

reading. This helps your child develop good listening and communicative skills, provides opportunities for him to hear the many sounds of language, and builds vocabulary. Show him the appropriate way to turn the pages. Follow the text with your finger as you explore and discuss the pictures. This helps him to distinguish between text and pictures, thus developing a concept of print.

Engage your child in conversation during all of your activities together. Help him expand his thoughts and language with who, what, where, and how questions. For instance, "What do you think we should do next? Where are they going?" Asking questions not only helps your child to develop vocabulary and thinking skills, it also assists him with reciprocal communication and joint attention skills.

Discuss topics that are not immediately present but involve knowledge about the world. This is an excellent way to encourage your child to think about language and the world around him. Help him draw from his current vocabulary and to add new vocabulary. This is a valuable practice for encouraging expressive language.

Repeat reading familiar stories to build familiarity and increase the likelihood that your child will want to attempt to read books on his own.

Participate in activities which increase your child's knowledge of the sounds of language by playing games, listening to music and by practicing finger plays that involve the identification of rhyming words, alliteration (several words that begin with the same sound), and matching sounds. These types of activities help to develop vocabulary, phonemic awareness, listening skills, alphabet recognition, expressive language and letter-sound correspondence.

Encourage writing in everyday play. For instance, pretend to take an order while playing restaurant. Make signs for a store front or advertisements for the restaurant. This is a wonderful exercise for emergent writers because they become aware of print concept, alphabet knowledge and letter-sound correspondence.

Look for words, letters and icons in your environment and point them out to help your child make meaning of letters and words. For instance, point out fast food signs and icons (the McDonald's arches, etc.), signs for restaurants, shopping malls, menus and street signs. This also helps your child develop a concept of print and alphabet awareness.

Let your child see you read. Read the newspaper, magazines and books. Children LOVE to pretend that they are "grown up" like you!

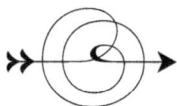

Our Advice To Parents About Language

Educators often have plenty of advice to offer parents about things they "should be doing at home" with their children to help with their language development. At times parents must feel frustrated by the advice. Often, families with whom we work expect or hope that their children will begin to speak, or learn to speak more clearly, simply by being in our classrooms.

Yet, as we have shared in this book, we hope that parents will see that language development is a process that takes time, and it happens wherever the child happens to be.

Language education begins at birth and the foundation for language is based on the rich culture, voices, discussions, stories, explorations and communicative exchanges that each child experiences, beginning within his own family. In the classroom we build with and upon this foundation, working to identify every child's unique needs and abilities while building their skills based upon what we understand about the complexities and nuances of language development.

Our advice to parents is to make language a first priority in their children's education. While you are helping them to develop their language at home, you are also preparing them to effectively communicate and share their unique thoughts and experiences with the world at large.

Enjoy the richness of life that comes from communicating with your children. And let's continue to talk about early language development as educators and parents.

References

American Speech Language and Hearing Association (2010). *Definitions of Communication Disorders and Variations.* Retrieved 12/16/2009 from: http// www.asha.org/docs/html/RP1993-00208.html

Baca, L.M., & Cervantes, H.T. (Eds.). (2004). The bilingual special education interface. NJ: Merrill/Prentice Hall.

Bardige, B. & Segal, M. (2005). *Building literacy with love: A guide for teachers and caregivers of children from birth through age 5.* Washington, DC: Zero to Three Press.

Beaty, J. (2002). *Observing the development of young children.* Upper Saddle River, New Jersey. Merrill Prentice Hall.

Bee, H., Boyd, D. (2007). *The developing child (11th ed.).* Pearson Education.

Brackenbury, T. & Pye, C. (2005). Semantic deficits in children with language impairments: Issues for clinical assessment. *Language, Speech and Hearing Services in Schools. 36* 5-16. American Speech-Language-Hearing Association.

Buffardi, J. (2009) *Atypical language development.* Power Point presentations, GMU EDSE 557. Fall 2009.

Buffardi, J., Keener, N. & Reasoner-Hill, L. (undated). *Phonological processes: A handbook.* An unpublished working manual. Fairfax, VA: Fairfax County Public Schools.

Center on the Social and Emotional Foundations for Early Learning (CSEFEL), (2006). Book nook. Using books to support social emotional development. Retrieved on 12/30/2009 from: http://www.vanderbilt.edu/csefel/booknook/ mondayrain/mondayrain2006.pdf

Clark, P. (2009). *Supporting children learning English as a second language in the early years (Birth to six).* Victorian Curriculum and Assessment Authority. Retrieved on 1/27/2013 from: http://www.vcaa.vic.edu.au/Documents/early years/supporting_children learning_esl.pdf

Encyclopedia on Early Childhood Development. (2009) *Language development, how important is it?* Retrieved on 12/28/09 from: http:// www.childrenencyclopedia.com/en-ca/language-development-literacy/ how-important-is-it.html

Genesee, F., Paradis, J. & Crago, M. (2005). *Dual language development disorders: A handbook on bilingualism and second language learning: Vol. 11. Communication and language intervention series.* Baltimore, MD: Paul H. Brookes Publishing Co.

Genishi, C. & Dyson, A. (2009). *Children's language and literacy: Diverse learners in diverse times.* New York, NY: Teachers College Press. Washington, DC: National Association for the Education of Young Children.

Gleason, J. (2005). *The development of language.* Boston. Pearson Press.

Goswami, U. (Ed.). (2004). *Blackwell handbook of childhood cognitive development* (5th ed.). Malden, MA: Blackwell Publishing.

Greenspan, S. & Wieder, S. (2006). *Engaging autism: Using the floortime approach o help children relate, communicate, and think.* Cambridge, MA: De Capo Press.

Hooper, S., Umansky, W. (2004). *Young children with special needs.* (4th ed.). Upper Saddle, NJ: Pearson/Merrill Prentice Hall.

Howley, M., & Arnold, E. (2005). *Revealing the hidden social code: Social stories for people with autistic spectrum disorders.* London: Jessica Kingsley Publishers.

De Houwer, A. (1999). *Two or More Languages in Early Childhood: Some General Points and Practical Recommendations.* Centre for Applied Linguistics. Available online at: http://www.cal.org/resources/digest/earlychild.html

Jennings, J., Caldwell, J. & Lerner, J. (2006). *Reading problems. Assessment and teaching strategies* (5th ed.). New York, NY: Pearson Education, Inc.

Koegel, R. L., & Koegel, L. K. (2006). *Pivotal response treatments for autism: Communication, social and academic development.* Baltimore, MD: Paul H. Brookes Publishing Co.

Leonard, Laurence B. (1998) *Children with specific language impairment.* Cambridge, MA: MIT Press.

Lifestrong. *Non-verbal communication in children.* Retrieved 1/2/2013 from web site: www.lifestrong.com.

Literacy Development, (n.d) *Literacy Development.* Retrieved on 1/09/2010 from http://www.mass.gov/Eeoe/docs/EEC/profdevelopment/literacydevelop menttraining.pfd

Lowry, Lauren. *Can children with language impairment learn two languages?* The Hanen Center. Retrieved on 1/19/2013 from: http://www.hanen.org/ Helpful-Info/Articles/Can-children-with-language-impairments-learn-two-l.aspx

National Research Council & Institute of Medicine (2000). *From neurons to neighborhoods: The science of early childhood development.* Committee on Integrating the Science of Early Childhood Development. Washington, DC: National Academy Press.

National Institutes of Health, (2013). *Selective mutism.* Retrieved 1/5/2013 from NIH's PubMedHealth website: http://www.ncbi.nlm.hih.gov/pubmedhealth/ PMH0002513.

National Institutes of Health, (2012) *Apraxia of speech.* Retrieved on 12/25/2012 from NIH's National Institute on Deafness and Other Communication Disorders website: http://www.nidcd.nih.gov/health/voice/pages/apraxia.aspx

Nekovei, D. L., & Ermis, S. A. (2006). Creating classrooms that promote rich vocabularies for at-risk learners. *Young Children, 61(5),* 90-95.

Nemeth, K., (2012). *Basics of supporting dual language learners: An introduction for educators of children from birth through age 8.* National Association for the Education of Young Children. Washington, DC.

Pepper J & Weitzman. (2004) *It takes two to talk. A practical guide for parents of children with language delays.* Canada. Hanen Center Publication.

Raines S, & Canady (1986). *Story Stretchers. Activities to expand on children's favorite books.* Beltsville,Maryland. Gryphon House, Inc.

Rocha, M., Schreibman, L., & Stahmer, A. (2007). Effectiveness of training parents to teach joint attention in children with autism. *Journal of Early Intervention, 29(2)*, 154-172.

Shulman, B. & Capone, N. (2010). *Language development: Foundations, processes, and clinical applications.* Sudbury, MA: Jones and Bartlett Publishers.

Stanton-Chapman, T., Justice, L., Skibbe, L. & Grant, S., Social and behavioral characteristics of preschoolers with specific language impairment. *Topics in Early Childhood Special Education, 27:2*, 98-109.

The Learning Triangle. (n.d). *Animals.* Retrieved on 2/5/2010 from http://willkids.org/pdf/Animals.pdf

Trawick-Smith, J. (2005). *Early childhood development: A multicultural perspective.* (4th Ed.). Upper Saddle River, NJ: Prentice Hall.

Volkmar, F. R., Paul, R., Klin, A., & Cohen, D. (2005). *Handbook of autism and pervasive developmental disorders: Assessment, interventions, and policy* (3 ed. Vol. 2). Hoboken, NJ: John Wiley & Sons, Inc.

Virginia Department of Education (2006). *Speech-language severity rating scales.* Retrieved on 1/2/2013 from website: http://www/doe.virginia.gov/special_ed/disabilities/speech_language_impairment/articulation_srs.pdf

Willis, C. (2006). *Teaching young children with autism spectrum disorder.* Beltsville, MD: Gryphon House Publishing.

Recommended Reading

Authors' Favorites:

Hirsh-Paskek, K., Golinkoff, R. & Eyer, D. (2003). *Einstein never used flash cards.* Rodale Press.
—This is a fun book for families on how children develop through play, daily exploration and experiences. Every pre-K parent should read this book to understand how much young children learn through their everyday experiences.

Nemeth, K., (2012). *Basics of supporting dual language learners: An introduction for educators of children from birth through age 8.* National Association for the Education of Young Children. Washington, DC.
—This is an easy MUST READ publication for families and educators of dual-language learners. It outlines the meaning of, strategies for, and the developmental stages of early dual language learners.

Pepper J. & Weitzman. (2004) *It takes two to talk. A practical guide for parents of children with language delays.* Canada. Hanen Center Publication.
—A MUST READ for families who wish to learn more about the importance of using easy, every day ways and basic strategies to encourage language development and communication in young children.

Reading is Fundamental (*RIF*) www.rif.org. National Headquarters—Reading is Fundamental, P.O. Box 33728, Washington, DC 20033. Phone: 202-536-3400 or 1-877-RIF-READ
—RIF is a literacy advocacy group. They provide an off-line and on-line reference center with the most current information on reading and literacy, as well as games and activities which encourage reading for all ages.

If you'd like more technical or detailed information, take a look at these:

Bee, H., Boyd, D. (2007). *The developing child* (11 ed.). Pearson Education.
— Psychology text book which outlines the developmental life of the child.

Center on the Social and Emotional Foundations for Early Learning (CSEFEL) http://www.vanderbilt.edu.
—An excellent website for families and educators to retrieve information on helping children develop social-emotional competence—an important piece in the development of pragmatic language.

National Institutes of Health http://www.nidcd.nih.gov
—NIH's website provides information on specific disabilities and developmental delays and provides information on speech and language impairments, disorders and delays.

Schickedandz, J. & Collins, M. (2013). *So much more than ABCs: The early phases of reading and writing.* Washington, DC: NAEYC.
—A book published by the National Association for the Education of Young Children (NAEYC) for early childhood professionals and their families which outlines what children need to learn, some strategies teachers can use to help them learn, and the various parts of emergent language and literacy which build the foundations for reading and writing.

About the Authors and Editor

Karen Griffin Roberts earned a Masters in Special Education, and a Bachelors of Individualized Study (BIS) in Early Childhood Development: A Study in Autism, from George Mason University (GMU). Her GMU undergraduate project to develop a manual for preschool teachers, which provided strategies for including children with autism in the classroom, won George Mason University's BIS award for "Most Creative Project" in May 2009. Worldwide response to the project from preschool administrators, special education and general education preschool teachers and families resulted in the publication of her book, *Embracing Autism in Preschool: Successful Strategies for General Education Teachers* (Fourth Lloyd Productions, 2010). Karen has taught preschool since 1992 and her teaching experience includes work with early childhood learning centers, day care centers and private preschool programs. In 1998 she was presented with the Children's World Learning Center's Honor Teacher Award and was one of eighteen preschool teachers chosen nationwide to attend the National Association for the Education of Young Children's 1999 Conference in New Orleans. She is currently an early childhood special education teacher for Prince William County Schools.

Ana Gamarra Hoover is a pre-school special education teacher in Prince William County, Virginia. She holds a Masters in Special Education degree with a concentration on Early Childhood Special Education from George Mason University (GMU). Ms. Hoover earned a Bachelor's of Independent Study in Child Development and Special Education also at GMU. She was awarded the academic award for the College of Education and Human Development in Early Childhood Special Education in 2010. Prior to her current job, Ms. Hoover ran a successful early childhood education business for twenty-three years. Ana lives in Burke, Virginia, with her husband, youngest son and four dogs.

M. Jean Buffardi earned an undergraduate degree in Speech Pathology at Kansas State University, a masters degree in Speech Pathology at the University of Pittsburgh, and certification in Early Childhood Special Education after additional graduate studies at George Mason University. During her 20 years with Fairfax

County Public Schools (FCPS) as a preschool special education teacher and speech/ language clinician for children 2-5 years of age, she also presented continuing education workshops on a variety of aspects of communication disorders and interventions for preschool children. She taught typical and atypical language development in early childhood as an adjunct instructor at George Mason University. She continues to provide early intervention services (birth-3 years of age) in Fairfax, Virginia, as a speech language pathologist. Prior to her work with FCPS, she taught preschool deaf and hearing impaired children in Prince George's County, MD.